Vow of Intimacy

Bond of True Love

D1595747

Bridget Ford

Soul. Truth. Love. Poetry. LC

ISBN: 978-1-7379689-1-7

First paperback edition April 2022.

Cover Photograph by KB Photography

Soul. Truth. Love. Poetry. LC
poemstellthestory@gmail.com
www.poemstellthestory.com

To the love of my life.

Table of Contents

Acknowledgements

The cover of the book is my husband, who is not a model, but chose to be one for the front cover of my novel. Thank you for helping me make my vision a reality. Such a handsome and loving man who gives me different ideas and support when it comes to marketing. I also appreciate all the feedback you have given me throughout this process. Thank you so much, Nivek Ford, for all that you do to help my dreams come true.

Isaiah Ford is my little muse. You fill my heart with so much joy I feel like my heart could explode at any moment. Thank you, my little baby, for being here with me. Thank you for loving me. You are everything I knew I needed. I love you forever and always baby boy.

Where do I begin with you? Such a long and growing relationship it overwhelms my heart. You are the friend I never knew I needed until I found life to be challenging without you. You spent so much time and energy in helping me make my dreams come true. Moments that will forever be appreciated. My push and drive that doesn't allow me to quit. You are a blessing God placed purposely in my path that I pray will never leave. The content, the design, editing the book, my mindset all goes back to you. Thank you so much for the time and the years and the love Treyvon Brunson.

A new star in my life that shines as bright as the biggest star near the moon. You are such an inspiration, a beauty, and an amazing friend that I am so blessed to have. I hope and pray everyone on this earth has a relationship like ours. You are my blood sister despite genetics. I wish I met you sooner. Thank you for the love, support, suggestions, book editing, and assistance during this process. I love you more than you know, Maranda.

Thank you to all my friends and family who continue to support me as a writer and poet. I love you all so much and appreciate every phone call, feedback, and all the support you all have graciously shown me. Thank you from the deepest part of my heart. I love you all so much.

Disclaimer

All poems are not based on personal events.

Bridget Ford

Introduction

Welcome to Vow of Intimacy

Welcome to my life. Welcome to my heart. Welcome to the love that tends to be withdrawn. I was a girl searching for happiness in a man that came with hurt. Searching for a peace that kept me out the dirt. A broken vessel lost in this life. That claimed love was the key when I no longer wanted to try.

Love is the tissue that dries your tears. Love is the blanket that comforts your fears. It was love that I sought and needed to survive. It was love that I mourned when peace told a lie. What defines me? So beautiful and smart. What controls me when I'm alone in the dark? The separation of that happiness every woman desire. That little taste of love that came in a unique form. The perfect man for you, who would walk in a glass room and place you on his lips. A forehead kiss to begin the mood. To show you his affection is quite clear and crude. Lost in love's perfection, that feeling we all pursue.

To the man of your dreams, the only love that was true. Seamless and perfect, from my heart you were chosen. Such a breathtaking love I grew weak to every moment.

A companion is what I wanted. A man was what I chased. Losing myself every inch of the race. A questionable love that broke. A woman who was a joke. Trying to find love with a fractured spirit. Searching for stability in relationships that failed to thrive. Hoping for a man to dry my eyes. A broken woman who chased love nonetheless, a beautiful woman who saw herself as less.

Come closer to me. Touch the bend in my back. Hear the shake in my breath. Feel the scars on my lips. A forbidden kiss that was rarely dismissed. To the man who was not my husband. To the man who was never chosen. My journey to my true love was dismantling, but worth it.

Twisted Affection

Floating in a river that doesn't seem to end.
Looking at the mountains that once didn't exist.
A peace you have to find to navigate your life.
A love that must die for peace to be mine.

The big blue sea with the sand beneath my feet.
Me at the bottom, sleep was retrieved.
Lifeless to the battle I continue to fight.
Push for the peace I'll find in due time.

A pond so small it's lonely and cold.
A frog on her lily pad auctioned to be sold.
Paid to the highest bidder for no fee at all,
A slave to my master, my boyfriend or boss?

How could this be? A person like me?
So lost in a world that has what I need?
A mother, a friend, a love that won't bend.
As strong as a twig lost in the wind.

I am here,
In a world so cold.
I am alive though my breath won't show.

You saw me in the river.
You heard me in the sea.
The pond though secluded you failed to notice me.

When I was the biggest.

You could see me from the stars.
Visible in the present, yet a deaf ear was drawn.

Tears soaking wet.
Death wish at best.
Trapped in a love,
Greed has possessed.

Bridget Ford

Chapter 1: Falling In Love

Man of my Dreams

To be in the arms of you.
To kiss you when you snore.
To watch you breathe every night,
Every piece of you adored.

You are the love of my life.
The one I can't ignore.
The one that helps me up.
The man I prayed for.

To get lost in your presence,
Leave me breathing in a dream.
You're my light and my love,
You're everything I need.

Bridget Ford

As my body laid on the blanket strategically placed on the moistened grass. I peered at the sky and got lost in the clouds. I thought of my knight and shining armor. The man I couldn't live without and I stayed in that moment. Time grew old. The sky greeted the moon. There was just me awaiting the man of my dreams. Longing for the moment my body goes weak.

Perfect for Me

Hold my body close,
Rock my mind to sleep,
Let me listen to your heart,
As it moves to every beat.

I love you my love,
A beautiful man like you.
You're everything I need,
My peace in a crowded room.

You are the love of my life,
A feeling most ignore,
But I'm here and I listened,
A love I now explore.

Your smooth brown skin,
Your big brown eyes,
The curve in your back,
My crush for a lifetime.

Can't you tell I love you?
Can you feel it in my lips?
The perfect man for me,
Your presence is a gift.

Bridget Ford

My ear to your chest. My fingers what's next. As it gracefully encircles your body and glides down your chest. A love I can't ignore. A love I must explore. Such a beautiful man in front of me. Beside me. Between me. Such a handsome man whose body surrounds me. A protective graceful love that lets me know I matter, through the lips of silence. A tangible love I can touch. I can feel. I can hold. Elegantly lost in the ambiance of your presence.

"I'm Falling for You"

A smile that competes with the sun,
Lost in the arms of the clouds,
As close as the planet near the moon.
"It's me, I'm falling for you".

Every moment is filled with memories,
Every thought identifies your touch,
Captive to the grip of trust.
"It's me, I'm falling for you".

Two bodies against the world,
Fearless, ready to explore,
The journey that starts with this moment.
"It's me, I'm falling for you".

I'm falling in a world without end,
Falling in love with my best friend,
A beautiful feeling, Love's first kiss.
"It's me, I'm falling for you".

Bridget Ford

*You are right here in front of me. A man I can see. A man I
can touch. The same man from my dreams. The man that
makes me blush. My hands begin to shake. My legs begin to
bend. This feeling that engulfs me, polish a love I can't resist.
Your presence. Your kindness. Your touch that surrounds me.
Makes me want to lose control and allow you inside of me.*

I'm supported by a feeling I can't see. Floating on intimacy. A feeling of ecstasy. Breathing a moment I want to last forever.

Mutual Love

What is love to a quiet kiss?
What is love to a gentle touch?
Body to body,
Skin to skin,
You wait for the moment you no longer pretend.

Lost in your eyes,
Caught by surprise,
The soft embrace of love,
A tantalizing design.

One word from you,
A sentence or two,
"I love you" so new,
So fresh,
So smooth.

One word or two,
The love that I knew,
Is now in my hands,
"I do love you too".

Bridget Ford

The best day in the world. Just me and you. Two bodies. Two
hearts. Alone in one room. We sat and we learned each
other's hidden truths. The ones no one can see when they're
looking at you. We dived much deeper than the clothes and

the shoes. We went past the surface. A sophisticated mood. When you remove the clothes and what's left is each other. The thoughts and the love that brought you together. You're left in a room naked to the truth. The words that you knew came and dictated the room. "I love you", so simple yet a demanding phrase. Dominated the moment, true love was displayed.

A Beauty in Time

Let me rest beside you,
My body to yours.
Let's get lost in the moment,
True love we must explore.
Time got us here,
Through time I understand,
The beauty of a man,
Rest in the lines of my hands.
A high I now can reach.
A passion you share with me,
True love I couldn't believe,
Enhanced the beauty you see.

Bridget Ford

Time so precious, so unique, and relentless. Time so pure, ongoing, and senseless. What brought me here to pass the time that was mentioned? Time kept me still. A love that was strengthened. The beauty of you woven through time, became the love of my life a feeling I can't deny or dismiss or release. A love full of peace, allows me to breathe. My person. My truth. My star past the moon. The radiance in your love, a love I'll never lose.

It's Natural

The perfect day.
The perfect hour.
Lost in your presence,
The perfect honor.
Such a beautiful day to get lost in your love,
An unspeakable feeling the grace of a dove.
When the sky started to gray,
And the stars lit up the sky,
This moment I knew,
This love came once in life.
The gentle touch when you never spoke,
The silence in the distance invoke,
An authority that dictated that very moment.
That beautiful day.
That perfect hour.
A peace in love that paraded the room,
As it watched our figures grow clueless to the moment,
That beautiful moment, that priceless day,
That left me completely in love with you.

Bridget Ford

Lost in a moment time couldn't predict. Floating in a love I once had to pretend. This man in-front of me made my legs shamefully shake. His love and his presence made my mind misbehave. I laid on his chest. His hands caressed my thighs. We laid next to the sun, as we closed our eyes. A peace that invoked from one simple kiss. One countless moment. An emotion so bliss. We laid with each other. My body to yours. With your lips to my cheeks, a feeling explored. The songs from the speaker and the love that implored left me drowning in ecstasy, unlike nothing before.

Lost in You

Alone in my eyes,
Let it catch me by surprise,
I'll let you love me from the top of my head to the sole of my
feet,
Love all of me,
Even the frustration in between,
Allow this love to make your soul go weak.

Bridget Ford

*Can I bask in this feeling forever? My king. My love. Can I
remain in this moment? Just you and me? A love that runs
deep. Your actions agreed. Down on one knee, he smiled and
proceed, "You are the love of my life. Will you marry me?"*

Chapter 2: I Do

Lights. Camera. Action.

The gown,
The dress,
The songs,
The vests.

First glance of my skin perfectly positioned with the sun.
The laugh that we share when you almost choose to run.
A small drip of icing a moment the camera stole.

I love you my king,
You showed me your love.
With no words at all,
It spoke in your touch.

The gowns,
The dress,
The songs,
The vests.

Could all disappear,
This moment's what's left.

Lost in your love,
My then and my now,
Love me forever,
Not the songs and the gown.

Just me, my brown skin, and my beautiful curves.
My thick plush lips give you the kiss you deserve.

me and the laughs that my silliness invites,
The smiles and the hugs, the moments that I cry.

Love me for who I am,
Not the songs and the dress.
Take the concert away and our bodies what's left.
You and me against the weakness in time,
A love that'll last forever even when the moment dies.

Bridget Ford

*The band fades in the distance. The moonlight kisses the
darkened sky. The torches and the candles light up the
moment. As I gaze into your eyes and you fall deep into mine.
We remember what brought us to this moment. Years ago,
when our conversations ran throughout the night. As I
learned you and you learned me. The person whose body is
patiently pressed up against mine, as we slowly sway with the
tunes of the soul band. I fell in love with the person, a
beautiful man. I fell in love with the man behind the smile. I
fell in love with your goofiness, your nonchalant behavior,
your thick nose, and your huge brown eyes. Such the perfect
man for me.*

Affection

As your hands grip my waist,
And your fingers display my smile.
As your eyes pull me closer,
My heart begins to pound.
Your smile shows my reflection,
The love amongst the crowd,
The energy that evokes,
The love that holds me down.
So powerful, can't you see?
The affection in-between.
Is a burst of light that beams,
Burns my insecurities.
You showed me, though I knew.
The love you shared is proof.
Is now a love that's tangible,
To know, not assume.

Bridget Ford

Your body around mine. Your touch so divine. As you caress my body with your love. A moment undefined. A moment you can't predict. My toes to your lips. A moment so serene that surpasses every wish. I can feel it in your touch. I can hear it in your silence. The intimacy in this moment has already been established.

Insightful Gestures

It's the little things you do,
That keeps my heart in love.
House chores.
Our children.
It's the simple things adored.

Present in the moment,
Just as powerful as a hug.
It's the small priceless gestures,
That makes me fall in love.

Cooking, cleaning, the things that some ignore,
Is the small kiss of love that makes my body warm.
The love from your gestures,
This service assures,
Are the simple acts of love that hits me at my core.

Bridget Ford

*My protector. My love. The man that keeps me standing.
Despite the obstacles we face, you are my right hand, each
and every day. Come closer to me baby. Let me show you
how much I care and adore the support you've shown, that
seems to be quite rare. Let me put on something nice. Come
into our room. Just relax on the bed as I come closer to you.
My body next to yours. You tell me what to do.*

Quality Time

I want to be with you.
Every second of every minute.
The time I most desire,
Your presence, the richest.
Time with you is a dream,
A moment stuck in time.
We'll laugh,
We'll kiss,
We'll talk and touch,
Your space is what I desire.
Intimate time with the man I love,
The only man I see.
To be lost in you,
Your lust,
Your smile,
Your presence is all I need.

Bridget Ford

From sunrise to sunset lets grind the sands of time. Let me learn more of you and get lost in your eyes. Let my body please you like we're guarded by snow. Baby focus on me. From my head to my toes. Pay attention to the message as I lick my moist lips. Precious time with my man is time well spent. Let me study you baby from inside and out. What makes you you? What makes you pout? What makes your body smile from a moment in your past? Just you and me baby, a love that will last. Explore the curiosity with the love of your life. Enjoy every minute, valued intimacy of the mind.

Mental Stimulation

You listen, you're here.
A moment so tantalizing,
A love so rich.
A receptor of your words,
Your tone,
Your speech.
The topic you pick always excites me.
The passion that moves like a rock skipped at sea.
The ripples it creates stimulates the chemistry.
A stimulating debate,
Love whispered my name,
A love of the mind,
I'm forced to behave.

Bridget Ford

My body began to shake. I started to break a sweat. I repositioned my body as your words danced through the phone and touched my chest. My focus was challenged. My love I had to manage. As you laid my body near the fireplace and caressed me with your words. With your speech, mental enlightenment an attraction that's unique. To make me fall in love with you almost effortlessly.

Protector

More than what I had in life.
Blessed to see the growth in time.
Pleased to meet a relationship unknown,
"I want my daddy", I stopped and froze.

Those nights I cried for a stranger nonetheless,
"I want my daddy!", the proof's in my chest.
My heart raced.
It ran past the truth.
A boot to my flesh? No, that isn't abuse.

I was very young. A nuisance at best.
I told the world he loved me though it rattled my chest.
Love rested in his swing, yes real love is invested.

The fear when he yelled.
The disdain he shared.
His eyes pierced mine.
"I'm in Hell. I could tell."

The devil himself. No father to me.
These thoughts burnt my soul as I dropped to my knees.
My child's innocence has been maintained.
He wanted his daddy and his father really came.
With a smile on his face and a charge in his step,
Love was establishing, that came without regrets.

This love is so nice it complements his smile.
A pride so pure it challenges the clouds.
No tears to stay.

No pain at all.

An imperfect man,
But a man just the same,
Allowed my son to dissect his father as a man not the name.

Bridget Ford

*Protector. Lover. Friend. Peace. All of these attributes
describe the man in front of me. A father to my son, in a way
that shows. His love and his scars, authenticity exposed. The
flawed crown of a King, yet a man just the same. Allows his
child to see the love behind the words of a name. A new
found love I truly can't explain.*

Selfless Love

A love that'll grow throughout the sands of time.
A love that will last,
Your body into mine.
To just be with you as time grows old,
To just laugh and dance,
No matter where time goes.

I am lost in the memories that stole my heart away,
Blind to the selfishness that lets me know my place.
Yes, I'm lost in the way my soul fell into you.
I'm seductive to the moments when all I have is you.

Take my love in marriage,
Let me love you past the end.
A love I never knew exist,
Too thick to comprehend.

A love that makes my mind grow weak,
I lose the words to say.
Love me til the sky grows old,
A life with you won't fade.

Lay me by the highest star,
My lips to yours embraced.
Love me like the selfish man,
Whose love is on display.

Bridget Ford

The tears ran down my face as I looked you in your eyes. You are my husband, a moment I've desired. We stood in the stars and the crescent of the moon. I grew weak to this moment, a love so true. Your hands graced my face as you pulled my body close. My big brown lips kissed your cheek as time began to froze. The love of my life is here in my hands. Your body, your love I can now understand. A love so deep that you lose the words to say and get lost in the moment. That intimate embrace. Maxwell's voice softly whispered into the night. Your love gracefully and purposely began to intertwine with my delight.

Chapter 3: Turbulence

Show Me You Love Me

Do you know I love you?
Can you tell I care?
Right beside each other,
And it's like you're never there.

I want to be beside you,
Hold me in your arms,
I know you said you love me,
Yet it feels like something's wrong?

Listen to my body as my words have now fade.
I need you to pay attention,
Focus! Find the words to say!

I love you, I told you time and time again,
But those are just words that slide between my lips.
Actions are the breath of life that makes it all real.
Your actions show me different,
Listen! I need you to be still!

Listen to my body when it shakes throughout the night,
Pay attention to the silence that starts a silent fight.
I just want you to hear me when I don't make a sound,
I just want you to love me, make me never have a doubt.

Bridget Ford

Silence strikes the night. Fear enters the room. Is it a
woman? Is it me? What makes you so distant and rude? I

showed you I love you in every way I can. I've told you I need you in a way you'll understand. What more can I do to be visible to you? I am here. I am present, yet alone in the room! A body to you that sleeps in the night. Am I someone you once loved, a love now out of sight? Look at me baby. Find the truth in my eyes. Assure me as I trust you, despite the jagged lies. Just show me you love me. One step at a time. Find the love that brought you here. I just need you to try.

Flawed Perfection

A love that's been sustained,
A teenage love that'll never change.
The first man to show me my beauty,
In a way I've never seen.
From the dazed gaze that showed as your eyes rested upon
my skin,
Or the boyish smile you gave that passed as a cocky grin.
I was your everything, before I knew my worth.
I was your love upon a time before love hurt.
We spent our time in laughs and smiles,
We had an affection that reached the clouds,
Hand in hand,
Heart to heart,
A dashing small unit, a love that sparked,
You made me see my beauty,
You showed me my worth.
The time you spent with me,
Was always guaranteed,
Despite the inconvenience,
You made sure I did believe,
The love you had in your heart,
Was truly meant for me.
I am the Queen you first created,
Back then I had no doubt,
That I would love you forever,
A love that stains the clouds.
Put me in a moment when affection was our sound,
You pulled my body close and placed my first crown.

Bridget Ford

A love that was secure. Though childish and young. A love that put me first. A bullet to a gun. He made the crown that now sits on my head. He straightened my gown and loved me instead. A dream in my hands. A queen to a prince. My youth I can't ignore, a love that was rich. He gave me my wings in a way I have adored. He loved me so loud, it hit me at my core. The beauty you see now came with some help. Some love. Some peace. That I didn't get myself. A boy from long ago that captured my heart in a way that'll never grow. He is why I know my worth. Take heed to this lesson. I WILL PUT MYSELF FIRST! To love me is a blessing.

Broken Promise

To death do us part is the promise I made.
Til God brings me home is the agreement I saved.
I said I would love you until I can't open my eyes.
I promised that I'd be there despite the battle in time.

I promise I love you, though now it's not the same.
The promise I made long ago is a feeling that has changed.
My husband. My friend. The father of my kids,
Has grown to be a cheater, a sin unforgived.

You forgot the vows you sung that day?
With your family and friends you told me you'd stay?
Through thick and thin.
Sickness and health.

You told me you loved me!
This I won't accept!

You lied!
You cheated!
You broke that one promise!
That we both stood in agreement,
A new bond established.

No need to be sorry,
No need to pretend,
I can see in your eyes,
You made peace with this sin.

Bridget Ford

Betrayal! Lies! Deceit! "How could you do this to me?! I trusted you with my love! I trusted you with my pain. Instead of loving me, you parade my insecurities!" The anger ran up my spine and burst in my eyes. I could feel my body shaking. I could hear my voice cracking. I was beyond pissed. The man I know and love didn't think I was enough. Shame echoed throughout my speech. So many feelings flooded my mind. "Do you not know how much I love you? Or you just don't care?!" Thump! I watched his phone helplessly hit the hardwood floor. "Goodbye", I muttered as I sprinted to the door.

The Years?!

You don't love me,
I can feel it in your lies.
The silence.
The tone.
The disconnect in your eyes.
I've done all I can do to right the wrongs, I've tried.
I promise I'll love you more than I ever have in life.
You're angry,
Upset,
And I don't understand.
I know life came with challenges, but this wasn't the plan.
My dress?
My love?
Our kids?
My friend?!
Do you see what you're doing?
Our life.
The years?!
Don't throw it all way,
Just stay Baby,
I'll do all I can,
To save our family.

Bridget Ford

*Listen to me at least one time. Dismiss the lust that scolded
your eyes. We are a family, let's not forget. We have too
much time invested in this. Love me or hate me, you're here
to stay. Your pride and lies will not cost me my name! What*

can I do to make you want to stay? A love and lust that ended in shame, only for me. Death would agree. A love like this shouldn't be retrieved. Yet here I sit. Here I stand. Defending your honor though you demolished the plan. And respect. Your greed was amateur at best. Why destroy our bond over meaningless sex?

A Beauty Like Me

The night is still,
The babies are sleep,
Yet my mind continues to race against the possibilities.
The possibility of love taking my hand.
The vision of trust
One day they'll understand.
I am who they see,
Those who cry out for peace.
It's you.
No me.
I can't wait to be free.
Free from uncertainty.
Free from the pain.
Free from the love,
Hidden in shame.
Free from the mistakes that haunted my past.
Free from the love that lies limp in my hands.
I'm living a life I can't truly claim.
Lost in a love that welcomes the rain.
How could this be? A beauty like me,
Lost in a world blind to defeat.
I am who you see,
Those who cry out for peace,
A beauty like me, in a love I can't leave.

Bridget Ford

My broken body laid across the bed numb to defeat. You
could see the tears that tatted my face. Dried but still present.

Peace must be late. I heard what he said. I know who he chose, but he still loves me. This must be a joke. So much time has passed. The history we share. A love that is flawed, a love that is rare. Til death do us part were the vows you broke. Drowning in misery, the truth won't revoke.

Toxic

Love is all that's left,
Like a kiss of death,
We now welcome the end,
A toxic relationship that shouldn't exist.

A love that had strings,
A chosen victim caught in flames,
Alive and vibrant,
Who never feels a thing.

Black suit and tie, aged death we can't deny.
A toxic love full of beautiful lies.
Lies that kept love to my lips,
A kiss I miss,
My chosen soulmate who's now dismissed.

Bridget Ford

Goodbye pain and anguish. Goodbye uncertainty. Goodbye love's first promise. Goodbye fake loyalty. Goodbye to the first man that made me smile. Goodbye to my first love who tried to right the wrong in doubt. Goodbye to the lie that made me fall in love. Goodbye to the kiss of hope that burnt my flesh and shrugged. Goodbye to the man who made me walk away. I loved you with everything, but that ends today. Focused on my baby, the man I know behaves. Here's a pencil or pen, just please sign your name.

A Mother's Love

With a scream and a grin your presence was known,
You laid on my chest stretched across time froze.
My son, my love you made time stand still,
My one and new friend that made life surreal.

I stared at your feet that seemed as long as a man,
I watched as you smiled when you caught wind of my glance.
A small little human so cute and warm,
My small little son, a heart I could hold.

Give me a chance even when the sun no longer fights,
Let me steal your heart, after all you have mine.
Let me be the one who protects you from the storm,
Let me hold you close like I did when you were born.

From the end of time to now I will always love your smile,
Your heart, your love, the kiss that killed my frown.
You are my son. The light in the day.
You are my peace and my strength,
The push when I'm afraid.

Can't you tell my child?
I am a woman just the same.
I am your peace and your love,
My life for yours, I'd trade.

Love you Isaiah.

Bridget Ford

Vow of Intimacy: Bond of True Love

It's me and you my love. Mommy and son against the world.

Chapter 4: Trust

Addiction

I'm addicted to the thrill,
I'm addicted to the high,
The feeling of love that goes past the sky.
A love that pleads clueless to what's wrong and what's right,
It goes and keeps going until you're stuck in due time.
A permanent love that stays with the true,
A love that gets stronger despite the mood.
It can't be erased.
It'll never be replaced.
A prisoner to a feeling prone to misbehave.
Both aggressive and loving,
A feeling blind to lies.
The truth ends the fantasy,
The bliss over time.
Stop loving you,
I can't.
Can't hate you instead.
So I fall dumb to the love I may soon regret.

Bridget Ford

*Staring in the mirror that protects my truth. The loneliness,
the love, the dreams I once pursued. I sit and I watch the
pain in my eyes. The discomfort in my chest when he
presumes to tell a lie. I don't trust you, I don't think I ever
will. The pain I've been through makes this all seem surreal.
But the feelings you show allow me to feel. A moment in time
when life could stand still. A love out of mind. Present and
vibrant. A love so exhilarating it reinforces my glow. You*

make me feel safe. A trust I must persuade, cause you're just another man playing a dangerous game.

He Waited

Caught in a world I can't trust.
Waiting for the one to fill me up.
Emotionally,
Physically,
In every way I need.
Please be my peace,
Let your love cradle me.
Hold me against the heart that breathes in your chest.
Lay my body beside,
A love we both possess.
A love like this I can't explain,
An exotic love that's not the same.
It's personalized to the soul I'm tied,
Destined for the love it invites.
Unless I fail to listen,
Unless I fail to see,
The man in front of me,
Is whose waiting for me.

Bridget Ford

*Am I blocking my blessing? Using trust as a reason? Wait,
how do I know you care for me? How do I know it's true?
How do I know you belong to me? A love that won't be
moved. By a woman or thought, that'll drive us apart. How
do I know it's true? You are still a man who adores women. I
know you admire a few. I need to be sure, this is something
real. I won't survive that mistake again! My heart hasn't
recovered. Give me some time to dissect, the love you*

welcome in without a single regret. Though true love has been a girl's first wish, last man who said he loved me made me lose my best friend.

Distant Love

Can you tell I miss you?
Can you feel it in the wind?
Can you tell I love you?
It's so strong I can't pretend.

That my thoughts don't flood with memories of you,
A dream that once exist,
A dream I once could touch,
True love I once could kiss.

Too far for you to touch me.
Too far to really see.
The love I had in front of me,
Is now a distant tease.

Come hold me in your arms,
Hear the heart I once could feel,
Touch the thoughts that kept me smiling,
Let me fall in love again.

Bridget Ford

Same city. Same climate. Same love. Different mindset. Blocked by the trauma in my past. A man who left his wife, despite the love we had. I still want you, I promise I do. My ex-husband just keeps making me confused. You're so close, yet so far away. I understand if my indecisiveness is too much for you to take. Wait! No! I deserve happiness too! Despite the pain I've been through true love I will pursue. Come back to me baby. Lay your head on my thighs. I promise I will fix it. Give me a chance to make you mine.

I Want You Here

Can you be here before the sun begins to rest?
Can you stand beside me?
Don't rush, but do your best?

To be here before the sky no longer blinds my eyes.
Your fingers in mines,
Our toes in the sheets,
Your eyes on my beauty,
A moment so serene.

I need you here,
I know you miss me too.
A love so pure,
That it captivates the room.

Meet me in the morning,
When the sun opens its eyes.
I want you here beside me,
Your body next to mine.

Bridget Ford

My body began to shake, you're allowed to misbehave. A love that was brewing, I lose the words to say. A feeling so serene, you're body next to me. So close to my lips I could feel it when you breathe. My legs continued to rock. My lips never closed, as I soaked in your presence a moment time froze. Body to body sends a peace through my spine. Lips to lips, see the lust in my eyes. You are who I've waited for

*since before my heart could see. The affection that
accompanies true love I now conceive.*

Love to the Test

Love is complicated,
This we know.
It's pain, love, and sex,
A feeling uncontrolled.

It grabbed me from my peace,
And gave me a release,
That allowed me to see,
The truth behind the tease.

I know you love me.
I can feel it in your touch,
I can hear it in your voice,
Your smooth brown skin against my body makes me blush.

I know I love you.
You can see it in my eyes.
I know that you care,
But love can be disguised.

Analyze the truth.
Put your feelings to the test.
Is it love or is the truth,
I'm the only one left?

Bridget Ford

The uncertainty in time is knocking at the door. Love can be built. True love can't be ignored. It's time I stop and choose.

The reason I pursued, the vulnerability that was clear before he entered the room. The time that we've spent. The memories we've made. Why did you pick me? Is this the plan you've made? I know time is whining down. It's a family you pursue. Just tell me the reason why I should spend my life with you.

Tick Tock

The fingers on the clock refuses to stop.
The sound that echoes each time it ticks and it tocks.
It calls my name with a silent smile.
It rocks me back and forth, then knocks me back down.

The beauty in time when you age like fine wine.
The mystery in your curves that form a fine line.
It's the sand in the glass that welcomes youth,
Each little piece forms an extravagant you.

The lust of time that makes us form a plan,
The dreams we chase before we run out of sand.
It's the beauty in the unknown that keeps us alive,
That same beauty that supports a hidden lie.

The luxury in time that will one day end,
A character so perfect it betrays a friend.
We love you when we love, we love you when we smile,
It's the box at the end that gives us those doubts.

Time is a mystery,
As mischievous as a clock.
It rests on the thoughts of you,
As it ticks and it tocks.

Bridget Ford

Time is a mystery, a path I must pursue. A blessing in
disguise, the question mark of you. Time keeps my mind

racing. Real love as motivation. To stop and embrace its beauty. The love that blows my mind. The joy that makes me cry. To bask in this feeling that breathes deep inside. The beauty of love in its one true form. The touch of a man before my body grows old. To look you in your eyes and feel a love so sweet. It tickles my soul. A love I now can be. Sits right here with me, so effortlessly. My one true love is no longer a dream. You, I can touch. You, I can feel. My one true love that makes life surreal.

Designated Happiness

Stuck in a dream,
A view I'd gladly take.
Fall in love with your person,
An addictive escape.

The love you're afraid to be,
Is the love you once believed,
The one you childishly labeled,
And hid it in your dreams.

Real love untamed,
Is now a person in your face.
The love that goes crazy when somebody says their name.

Lips and body next to yours such a beautiful escape.
I'd drown in this forever,
Euphoria everyday.

Different then what's hidden in a dream,
A love that's phenomenal,
What I never knew I need.

Hold it. Feel it. Let it overwhelm my heart,
For this love I feel is rarely seen,
I'll take it and restart.

Bridget Ford

It's my turn to love. It's my turn to be happy and allow love to consume me. I have been weary and broken of a love that was never true. A man who broke a promise and moved like it was cool. He neglected our future. Tainted our love. He failed to give me what I really wanted. An unwavering love that can be sustained. Despite the different obstacles that parade in our face. A love I thought would hit the clouds, failed to be maintained. And for that I am proud because you helped me find my one true love, who I can't live without.

Conclusion

Your love within my body. Your touch as you surround me.
Makes me hit the highest star, a feeling of ecstasy. Your body
on mine. This moment so right. As I hold you and caress you
a connection so divine. As your body shakes and rocks. True
love on top. I love you my king. A love that'll never stop.

True Love

True love's first kiss,
From the man you love.
True love's first touch,
Puts you in heaven above.

To hold you and love you a man in my arms,
Births a peace I can't explain,
True loves true form.

Destiny is our future,
Of which you can't control.
A love that will strengthen,
A love that grows old.

Your body, your skin
Your touch, your lips
Makes me numb to your presence,
A love I won't dismiss.

Take me in your arms,
Pull me close to you,

Lay me by the moon,
Let the stars guide the mood.

Let them be our light,
To navigate our truth,
Let them lightly touch our love,
A love I won't confuse.

Bridget Ford

About the Author

Bridget Ford is a hardworking mother, wife, Registered Nurse, and author. She is the author of the novel, "Strength Beneath the Scars", which is a book of poetry that discusses strategies she used to overcome feelings of depression. She includes 4 short stories to give the readers a descriptive depiction of some of the difficult moments she faced in her life. Ultimately, she began writing poetry at 16, but due to life's challenges she neglected writing for years. Once she obtained her Master's Degree in Nursing Education, she wrote her first book of poetry and began writing a large variety of poems that influenced her next few projects. She enjoys writing poems that depict a story. She uses imagery and metaphors to place you in a different setting without leaving your seat. You can find her previous novel and information regarding upcoming projects on her website at www.poemstellthestory.com. You can also keep up with future projects on her Instagram page (@poemstellthestory).

Craving More?

Stay tuned for my next book! We will uncover the struggles
that minorities continue to
face in the 21st Century! The battle didn't end with slavery!
We are still prisoners to a
world that was not framed to include pigmentation.

Two Faces

Never forget your history.
Never dismiss your past,
That breathed before your life ever touched God's hands.
We are black.
We are here.
And we are still fighting to be free.
Though the beatings aren't as frequent,
And the cries aren't as loud,
We're still cursed with the order to always bow down.
The decree to be less.
The plea that we are blessed.
Entertain the lies you'll fail the test.
You are me,
And I am you.
We both have to hide ourselves to be allowed in the room.
We are still beautiful,
Naked or clothed.
Never let too much pigment show.
Pretentiousness must be a trait you gloat when the doors are
closed.
Yes, success in the black community has been maintained.
Our colleagues understand,

Bridget Ford

We will never be the same.
Maybe later but not today.
Even our names have others afraid.
The intimidation that sparks before our foot greets the floor.
The fear that leaps when pigmentation is explored.
We carry our grace in a different way.
Because even today we are not the same.
We are still black and ashamed.
Ask the second face that also carries your name.

Bridget Ford

Made in the USA
Columbia, SC
15 March 2022

57468021R00046